Four-Legged Friends

A Story Collection

Contents:

The Ears of Mandy
Written by June Epstein 2

How Dogs and People Became Friends
An African folk tale, retold by Gail Saunders-Smith 10

Dick Whittington and His Cat
Retold by Janet Stott-Thornton 18

The Checker-Playing Hound Dog
An American Tall Tale, written by Joe Hayes 24

Illustrated by Melissa Webb

The Ears of Mandy

There was a fat, silvery cat who was so old that none of the children in his house could remember when he was a kitten. He was old before they were born.

He was called Mandy because someone mistook him for a girl cat, and by the time they found out he wasn't, it was too late.

He spent most of the day lying on the window seat in the livingroom, or on a cushion on the back porch. He was too old to be active, and his eyes were so bad that he could hardly see at all. But his whiskers twitched a lot.

And his ears! That cat could hear anything and everything. You might say he lived through his ears.

His ears told him when the day started, because he heard the birds begin to sing. Then he heard the *tring tring* of the alarm, the *creak creak* of the bed, the *patter patter* of small feet, and the *slap slap* of Somebody's slippers.

Click went the latch of the back door, *eek eek* went its hinges, and Somebody said, "Outside, Mandy!"

So out he went. When he was ready to come in again, he gave one meow at the back door.

Chink chink went the cups and saucers, *guggle guggle* went the milk as it was poured into his own special dish. *Purr purr* went Mandy, when he had finished his breakfast and wanted to say thank you.

He snuggled against Somebody's pajama leg, and a big warm hand stroked his fur, and he heard Somebody's voice say, "Good kitty." That was how Mandy's day always began.

But one morning a terrible thing happened. He heard the birds begin to sing while it was still dark. He waited for the alarm. There was no *tring tring*. He waited for the bed. There was no *creak creak*.

He listened for the *patter patter* of small feet and the *slap slap* of Somebody's slippers, but nothing happened.

All was quiet for a very long time. Then he heard footsteps on the path outside the back door. *Click* went the door, *eek eek* went the hinges, and a voice said, "Outside Mandy!"

Only it wasn't Somebody's voice. Mandy knew it belonged to the boy next door. Mandy would have refused to go outside, but he needed some fresh air.

When he was ready for breakfast there was another unpleasant surprise. His special dish of milk had been placed on the back porch instead of on the kitchen floor.

"Meow," said Mandy at the back door. But nobody opened it. Mandy was insulted.

He would have refused to drink the milk, but he was thirsty.

That was a terrible day. He couldn't hear his family at all. They had gone away. He couldn't get inside the house. He had to sleep all day on the cushion on the porch. Mandy would have refused to sleep, but he was old and tired.

At suppertime, the boy next door gave him some cat food, and later he let him into the house for a while. He even said, "Good kitty," and tried to stroke him. But his hand was so different from Somebody's that it made Mandy cross.

In fact, he would have scratched the boy next door if he had not been a well-trained cat who knew his manners. Besides, he was very old. The next day was just as bad, and the next, and the next.

On the next day after that, Mandy was lying on his cushion, listening to the cars swishing along the road and the people tramping along the sidewalk. Suddenly something wonderful happened.

From all the different sounds on the street, Mandy's ears picked out one particular sound. His whiskers began to twitch. It was the special *vrrrm vrrrm* that he knew came only from the engine of one special car. It was Somebody's car

Mandy listened. *Beep beep* went a horn, *slam* went a car door, *cling clang* went the gate. *Vrrrm, vrrrm* went the car along the drive, *slam slam slam* went the car doors, *chatter chatter* went the voices. And he knew that his family had come home.

Next day, Mandy woke early on his window seat in the livingroom. He didn't wait to hear the birds, or the alarm, or the bed, or the feet, or the slippers.

He forgot he was old and fat and slow. He went quickly *pit-pat pit-pat* into the bedroom, jumped onto Somebody's bed and snuggled down on the blankets. A big warm hand stroked his fur and Somebody's sleepy voice said, "Good kitty!"

Then Mandy made his own loudest, happiest, special purring noise, and it was everybody else's turn to listen.

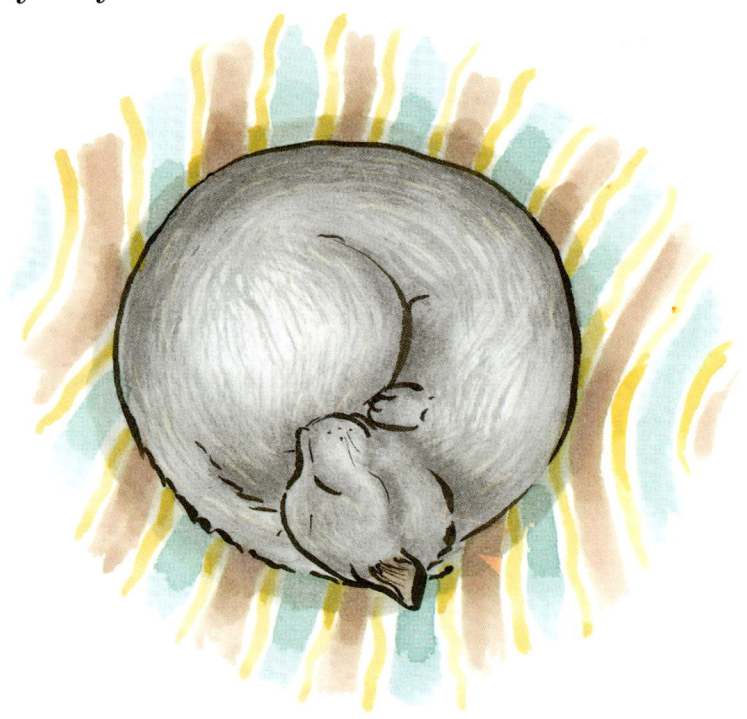

How Dogs and People Became Friends

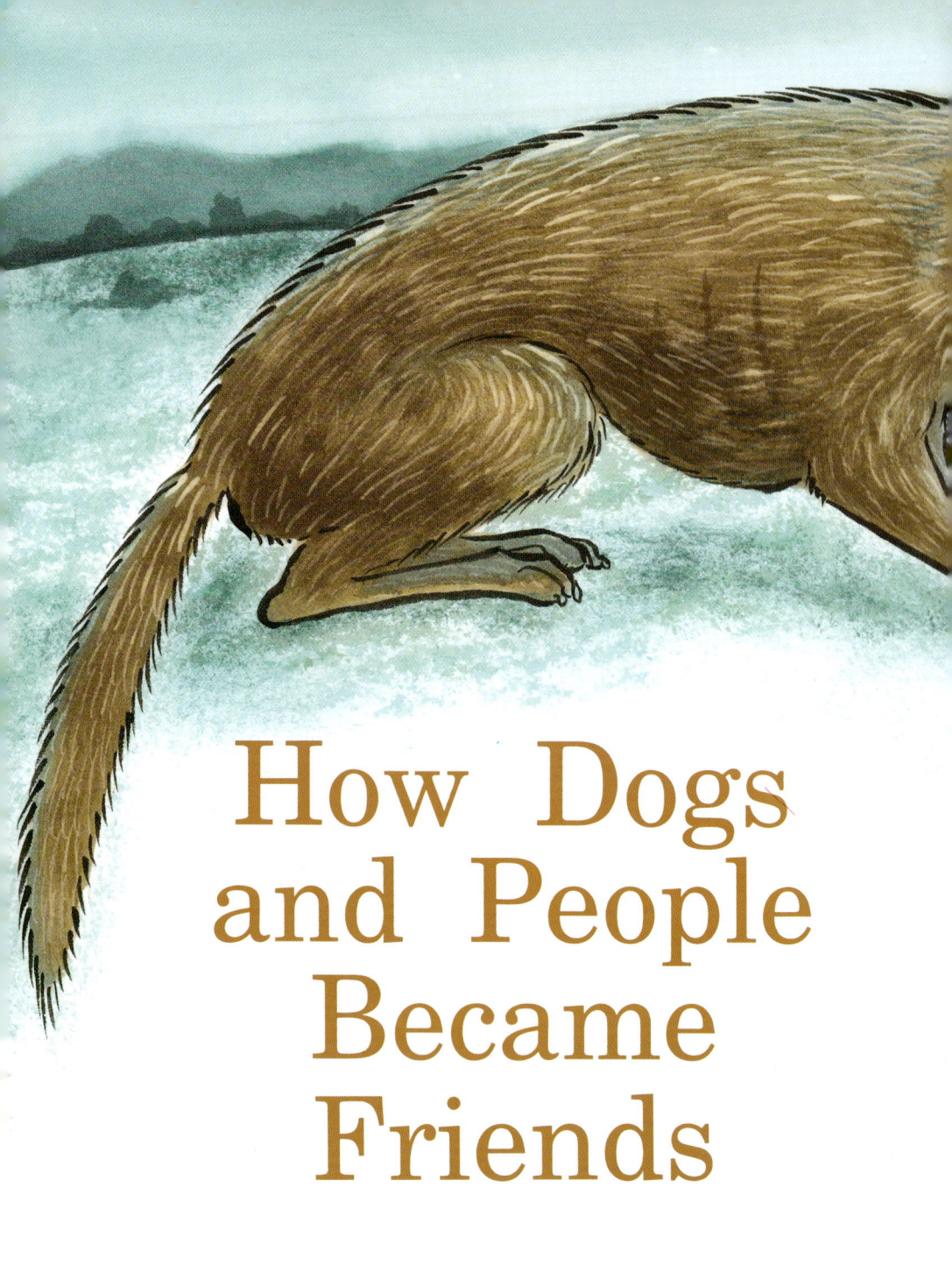

Deep in the jungle
lived the dog and the jackal.
Each day they ran together, hunting for food from sun up to sun down, and then huddling together for warmth at night.

One day they ran and hunted but caught nothing to eat. That night the wind was cold and their stomachs were empty, and together they shivered in the night air.

"I am hungry and cold," said the dog.

"I am too," said the jackal. "Go and find me something to eat. Bring it back and I will share it with you."

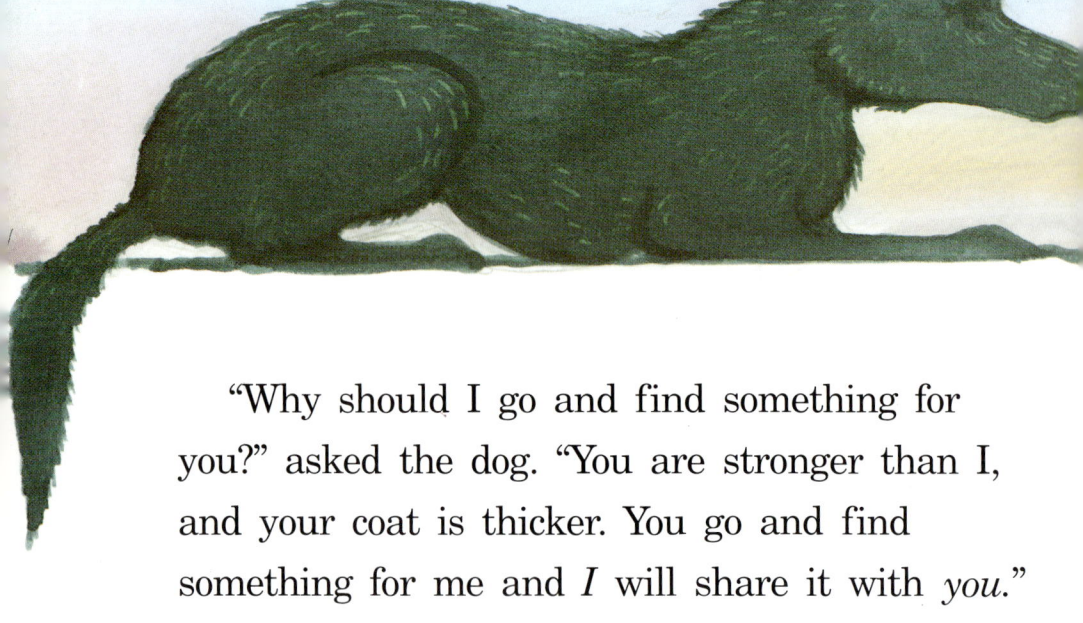

"Why should I go and find something for you?" asked the dog. "You are stronger than I, and your coat is thicker. You go and find something for me and *I* will share it with *you*."

"I will not go," said the jackal. "I'm too tired."

"And I will not," said the dog, who was too scared to go on his own.

So their stomachs continued to rumble, and neither animal could sleep. Then, long into the night, the dog noticed a fire deep in the jungle. "What makes that fire far off in the trees?" he asked.

"Oh, that fire comes from a village where there are people. Go to sleep."

"People?" The dog knew about people. Once he and the jackal had come upon a place where people had been, and they had eaten the bones and bits of meat that lay among the remains of the fire. The bones had been tasty, and the meat had been crisp and good.

"Do you think these people will have bones and bits of crisp meat?" the dog asked the jackal.

"I do not know. Why not go and see if they have any scraps? Go quietly, steal their scraps, and bring them back here."

The dog thought about this, and about how hungry he was, and he decided to go. "If I am not back soon," he said in a nervous voice, "call for me so that I can find my way back here."

The dog shivered with excitement and fear as he crept toward the fire. His heart was pounding. But as he came closer, the smell of meat filled the air and made his mouth water. Now that he could see the bones lying by the fire, he felt braver. Crouching low, the dog crept nearer the fire, and he carefully reached out with a paw to take a bone.

But the sudden movement disturbed the fire and sent up a galaxy of sparks.

"Who is trying to steal the fire?" one man shouted as he sprang from the shadows. The man raised his fist above his head, and the dog cowered in fear.

"Please," pleaded the dog, "I have not come to harm you or steal your fire. I have only come to eat your scraps and warm myself. Do not hurt me."

"Why should I not hurt you?" asked the man. "Tell me why we should let you warm yourself and eat our scraps. What will you do for us?"

The dog thought and thought. It was warm here, and there would always be food. People might be better friends than the jackal had been.

So the dog went on: "I will be your companion," he said. "I will never ask anything of you other than the warmth of your fire and the scraps that you do not want. For this I will travel with you during the day and sit by you in the night. I will warn you of danger and protect you from harm. I will offer comfort in your sadness and will join with you in play. Please, let me be your friend."

The man and the other villagers looked at the dog and talked quietly among themselves. Finally one said, "All right, you may stay." The dog and the people sat together in the warm glow of the fire that night and every night after that. They often heard the jackal howling in the night as he called out to the dog.

Sometimes one of the people would say, "Listen to that fool jackal howling in the night." And it seemed that the dog would smile.

Dick Whittington and His Cat

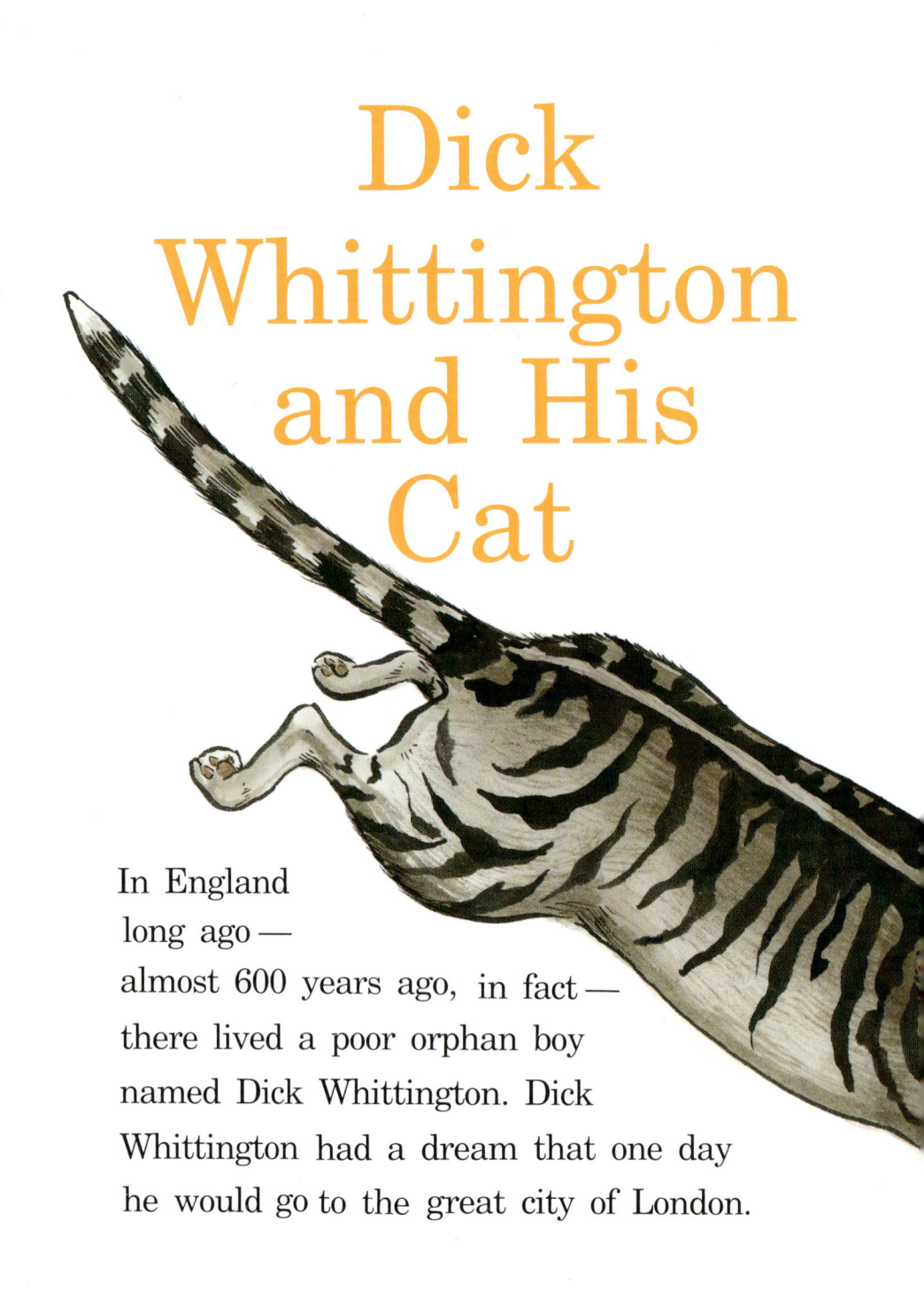

In England long ago — almost 600 years ago, in fact — there lived a poor orphan boy named Dick Whittington. Dick Whittington had a dream that one day he would go to the great city of London.

There, he had heard, the streets were all paved with gold.

Imagine Dick's disappointment, then, when he reached London at last and found that the streets were nothing but dirt and mud. Dick wandered through the city, hungry and tired, until at last he stopped outside a fine house and sat down to rest.

He was still there when the master of the house, a rich ship-owner named Mr. Fitzwarren, came home that evening. Mr. Fitzwarren saw that the boy was much in need, and he offered him shelter, a good meal, and a job in his kitchen.

Mr. Fitzwarren's servants did not give the poor country boy a warm welcome. They laughed at him and scolded him, and the bed that they gave him was in an attic where rats and mice squeaked and scratched all night.

Dick worked hard, however, and one day he earned himself some money by cleaning the shoes of one of his master's guests. It was with that money that he bought himself a cat, the best mouse catcher that he could have hoped for — and his one friend in the entire city.

One day Mr. Fitzwarren called all the workers of his household together. His ship, *The Unicorn*, was due to sail, and for good luck he wished each of his servants to put something of their own on board, to be sold in faraway lands.

When Dick's turn came, Mr. Fitzwarren said that as he had no other possessions he should send his cat. Unwillingly, but feeling that he could not refuse his master, the boy did as he was asked.

The other servants had seen the tears in Dick's eyes, and they made fun of him mercilessly until at last Dick was so miserable that he made up his mind to run away. He set off, running on and on until he reached the top of a high hill overlooking the city.

At the top of the hill there was a stone, and resting on this rough seat, Dick sat and pondered. And as he pondered, he felt so unsure of what might lie ahead that he changed his mind about running away.

He even managed to get back to work before anyone noticed he was missing.

The Unicorn, with Dick's cat on board, sailed away across stormy seas and at last arrived upon foreign shores.

There a great feast was prepared to welcome the strangers from England — and the smell of food attracted a great number of rats and mice.

The captain of *The Unicorn* was told that these vermin were a great problem in the land; indeed, the King would give a fine reward to be rid of them. Hearing this, the captain said that he had the very thing, and he fetched Dick Whittington's cat without delay.

The cat made such short work of the rats and mice that the King said he must have this precious creature for his own. He handed the captain a chest of jewels for payment.

Soon the ship returned to London, and the captain presented the jewels to Dick Whittington. They were worth a fortune — the poor country boy was suddenly a rich young man!

And as for Dick's cat: well, far away in a foreign land, this fine mouse-catcher lived the rest of his life like a king.

The Checker-Playing Hound Dog

When I was growing up, there was one man all the youngsters in our town admired. He was an old cowboy named Slim. He lived in a tumble-down shack on the other side of the tracks and every kid in town would go there to hear him tell about his experiences back in the days of open range cowboying. He'd talk about cattlemen and outlaws and horses he'd known.

Slim used to tell us, "Kids, the smartest thing on the range is a good cow pony. After that comes a sheep dog. And third in line is a man with a college education."

25

I wasn't so sure that was true, because Slim hadn't even finished the fourth grade, much less college, and he seemed to be the smartest man alive to me. But I had to agree that a dog can be smart. I had owned some pretty sharp ones myself. One of them was part retriever, and I think he was the smartest of them all.

Now, you may have seen dogs that can fetch back a stick you throw or play catch with a ball. Of course my dog could do all those things ever since he was a week old. But when this dog was full grown, he could understand anything I said to him and bring me whatever I asked for.

If I was playing down by the creek and got my feet wet, I'd tell my dog, "Go get me some dry socks." And in five minutes he'd be back with a pair of clean socks in his mouth.

Or if my friends and I decided to get up a ball game, I didn't have to run home and get my glove like the other kids. I'd just send my dog. Of course I'd have to tell him which one I wanted because I owned a fielder's glove and a catcher's mitt too. And he never once brought me the wrong one.

I was really proud of my dog and I thought he was just about the smartest dog there ever was, but I guess I found out different.

You see, one day I started bragging at school about my dog. I said I owned the smartest dog in town. A boy from across town said he'd bet his dog was smarter than mine. We bet a dollar apiece — and that was a lot of money for a kid in those days — and we set the next Saturday as the day for the contest.

When Saturday arrived I took some of my friends and my dog and went to the vacant lot where we agreed to hold the contest. The kid from across town showed up with his friends and his dog, and we got started.

First we had our dogs do the regular tricks — sit, shake hands, roll over, stand up on their hind legs. My dog did those things easily. And he could also stand on just his two left legs or his right legs. He never got left and right confused, either.

The kid from across town said that was nothing. He told his dog, "Go see if Ma's baking cookies." And he told one of my friends to go see if it wasn't true. Sure enough, my friend came back and told us the kid's mother was baking chocolate chip cookies. So I told my dog, "I'm hungry. Go get me an apple." He ran to my house and brought back a nice fat red apple in his jaws. He didn't poke any holes in it with his teeth, either.

"What do you say to that?" I asked the kid from across town.

"Nothin' much. Only watch this." Then he told his dog: "Go borrow Robert Sleaver's baseball." His dog ran down to Robert Sleaver's house and brought back the ball that was on the porch.

Now all the cross-town kids started saying that was the best trick of all. It's one thing for your dog to go to your own house and fetch something, they said, but it takes a really really smart dog to know which one of your friend's houses you're talking about and go there to borrow something for you. They started hooting and laughing and said their friend had won the bet.

But I wasn't licked by a long shot. I pulled a dollar bill out of my pocket and held it out to my dog. I told him, "Run down to Franklin's store and get me a pack of gum."

My dog snapped the dollar out of my hand and was gone down the street. He came back in no time with a little brown paper sack in his mouth. I opened the sack and showed everyone what was inside — a pack of chewing gum and ninety-five cents change. Now it was my friends' turn to laugh.

But the boy from across town said, "Wait a minute. How did your dog get the gum in the sack? And who gave him the change?"

I told him Miss Franklin at the store knew my dog and would always put the gum and change in a sack for him to bring back to me.

"That's cheating!" the cross-town kids all shouted. "Your dog had help."

"But he picked out the right gum," I argued. "I'll bet your dog couldn't do that." My friends all agreed with me and a big argument began.

Well, there was only one thing to do. We'd have to talk to old cowboy Slim and let him settle the argument. So we all headed down to his shack across the railroad tracks. When we got there the door was standing open so we trooped right into the kitchen. Then we all burst out laughing. There was Slim sitting at his kitchen table with a checker board in front of him. And sitting across the table was his big old flop-eared dog. And they were playing checkers!

Slim looked up from his game and gave us one of his slow, toothless grins. "What can I do for you kids?" he asked.

We all felt kind of foolish. "Well," we said, "we've been having a big argument about who owns the smartest dog in town. But you just settled it. Your dog is the smartest. He can play checkers!"

Slim kind of tipped his hat up and scratched his head with one finger. "Oh, he ain't so smart," he drawled. "I just beat him three games out of five."